TEMPTING

CHICKEN

COOKBOOK

Your Promise of Success

Welcome to the world of Confident Cooking, created for you
in our test kitchen, where recipes are double-tested by our team of
home economists to achieve a high stardard of success.

M U R D O C H   B O O K S®

Sydney • London • Vancouver

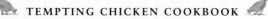

Not so long ago, chicken was reserved for special occasions. Only 40 years ago a person would eat a mere four chickens a year. Now each of us consumes about 22. Today we think little of buying a chicken to cook for dinner, regardless of whether there's any celebrating to be done! Supermarkets now stock ready-to-cook pieces like breasts, thighs, drumsticks, and wings, which make meal preparation quicker and easier than ever before. You can also buy already cooked barbecued and smoked chickens at many supermarket delicatessens.

Apart from taste attributes, chicken is a nutritious food which is high in protein, phosphorous, and niacin. Chicken is also a good source of iron. The breast section has the lowest fat content. For fat-watchers, be sure to remove the skin and trim off any fat before cooking.

All food should be handled and stored carefully to avoid food poisoning, but chicken requires extreme care. Fresh, uncooked chicken should be

WHOLE CHICKEN		
Small	2 – 2^1/$_2$ lbs	2 – 3 servings
Medium	3 – 4 lbs	3 – 4 servings
Large	4 – 5 lbs	4 – 5 servings
CHICKEN PIECES		
1 whole breast		1 serving
1 – 2 half breasts		1 serving
1 – 2 drumsticks		1 serving
1 to 2 thighs		1 serving
1 drumstick and thigh		1 serving
1 whole boned breast		1 serving
1 to 2 half boned breasts		1 serving
2 boneless thighs		1 serving
3 to 4 chicken wings		1 serving
COOKED CHICKEN MEAT (DICED)		
1 medium chicken		about 4 cups
2 whole breasts		about 2 cups
1 thigh and drumstick		about 1 cup
Allow ^{1}/$_2$ to ^{3}/$_4$ cup diced meat for each serving, depending on the other recipe ingredients.		

stored in the coldest part of the refrigerator for one or two days only. Make sure it is not in a position where it can drip onto other foods, causing cross contamination. Frozen poultry should be defrosted in the refrigerator before cooking. Never leave chicken on a counter at

room temperature to defrost because harmful bacteria can multiply quickly in a warm atmosphere. Frozen poultry should be brought home from the store as soon as possible and stored in the freezer. If the chicken has started to defrost, place it in the refrigerator and let it thaw slowly. Then you can cook it and refreeze it, if desired.

After handling raw chicken, be sure to wash your hands, the work surface, and any utensils with hot soapy water. Pay special attention to cutting

boards where small pieces of meat and juice can remain. Don't handle cooked and uncooked food together or use the same utensils in their preparation without washing them.

Chicken must be thoroughly cooked before eating. Pierce the thickest part of the flesh with a knife. The chicken is done if the juices run clear and the meat near the bone is no longer pink. If the juices and meat are still pink, continue cooking. Or, for a whole chicken insert a meat thermometer in the thickest part of the thigh. The bird is done if it registers 180° to 185°.

Cooked dishes that are not going to be eaten right away should be cooled quickly (immerse base of baking dish in ice water to speed things up) and placed in the freezer or refrigerator.

You'll find many

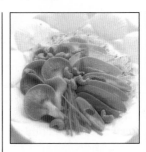

other handy tips for storing and handling poultry throughout this book. The recipes presented in this *Tempting Chicken Cookbook* have been inspired by the cuisines of many nations. The recipes are appropriate for a family dinner or a special occasion celebration.

Poultry Hot Line
For answers to your questions about poultry, call the U.S. Department of Agriculture's Meat and Poultry Hot Line. The toll-free number is 1-800-535-4555. (In the Washington, D.C. area call 447-3333.) Home economists at the hot line take calls from 10 a.m. to 4 p.m. eastern time.

Salads, Soups, and Starters

Chicken is one of the most obliging of foods, marrying well with a wide range of flavors. For salad dishes, use a dressing to coat the cooked meat. Or, poach the raw meat in a combination of herbs, spices, oils, and vinegars or marinate it overnight. The more inspired your choice of marinade and dressing ingredients, the more diverse your repertoire of recipes will be. Any one of the recipes in this section can be adapted to become a meal in itself. A terrine using richly flavored chicken livers is an excellent light main course when served with a salad. Soup becomes substantial fare when you accompany it with a hearty whole grain bread.

Spicy Chicken Salad

Preparation time:
  25 minutes
Cooking time:
  20 minutes
Serves 6

1½ pounds boneless
  skinless chicken
  breasts
1 tablespoon olive oil
1 onion, finely chopped
2 cloves garlic, crushed
2 teaspoons curry
  powder
1 teaspoon ground
  coriander

½ cup mayonnaise
½ cup plain yogurt
⅓ cup golden raisins
3 tablespoons French
  salad dressing

1 In a large skillet place chicken breasts and water to cover. Bring to a boil; reduce heat. Cover; simmer 20 minutes or till tender and no longer pink. Drain. Cool chicken.
2 Meanwhile, in a small saucepan heat oil. Cook onion and garlic in oil till tender. Add curry powder and coriander. Cook and stir for 2 minutes. Cool

Clockwise from top: Easy Chicken Vegetable Salad (page 6), Spicy Chicken Salad, Moroccan Chicken Salad (page 6)

to room temperature.
3 In a bowl stir together mayonnaise, yogurt, raisins, and salad dressing. Add onion mixture and stir till well combined.
4 Shred chicken and add to mayonnaise mixture, stirring till well combined. Cover and chill till serving.

Easy Chicken Vegetable Salad

Preparation time:
  25 minutes
Marinating time:
  30 minutes
Cooking time: None
Serves 6

2¹/₂- to 3-pound whole cooked chicken, skinned
3 carrots, peeled
8 ounces snow peas, trimmed
14-ounce can baby ears of corn, drained
1 red bell pepper, cut into small squares

Dressing
3 green onions, finely chopped
¹/₄ cup white wine vinegar
2 cloves garlic, finely chopped

1 tablespoon finely shredded gingerroot
1 teaspoon Dijon mustard
²/₃ cup salad oil
1 tablespoon soy sauce
¹/₂ teaspoon sesame oil
Freshly ground pepper

1 Remove meat from chicken; cut into bite-size strips. Place in a large bowl. Blanch carrots in boiling water for 3 minutes; drain. Place in a colander and rinse with cold water; drain. Bias slice carrots and add to chicken.
2 Blanch snow peas in boiling water 30 seconds. Rinse with cold water; drain. Halve corn lengthwise. Add snow peas, corn, and red bell pepper to chicken mixture.
3 For dressing, combine green onions, vinegar, garlic, gingerroot, and mustard. Gradually whisk in salad oil, soy sauce, and sesame oil till well combined. Pour over chicken mixture, tossing to coat. Season with pepper.
4 Cover and marinate in the refrigerator for 30 minutes. Toss again before serving.

Moroccan Chicken Salad

Preparation time:
  35 minutes
Cooking time: None
Serves 4

2¹/₂- to 3-pound cooked whole chicken, skinned
3 medium oranges
12 whole pitted dates, halved
6 radishes, thinly sliced
¹/₃ cup whole blanched almonds
2 tablespoons lemon juice
2 tablespoons olive oil
¹/₂ teaspoon ground cinnamon
¹/₄ teaspoon garam marsala (available at Asian markets)
Freshly ground pepper

1 Remove meat from chicken; cut into thin strips. Peel oranges and cut into thin slices.
2 In a bowl combine strips of chicken, oranges, dates, radishes, and almonds.
3 In a small bowl whisk together lemon juice, oil, cinnamon, and garam marsala till well combined. Pour over chicken mixture, tossing to coat. Season with pepper. Serve immediately.

HINT
Always remove bones and skin from cooked chicken pieces when preparing salads. Cut or shred the cooked chicken into neat, bite-size pieces.

Smoked Chicken Salad with Sweet and Sour Dressing

Smoked Chicken Salad with Sweet and Sour Dressing

Preparation time:
20 minutes
Cooking time: None
Serves 4 to 6

4 ounces salad sprouts
(see Note)
1 carrot, peeled and cut
into thin strips
5 ounces oyster
mushrooms (see Note)

5 ounces snow peas,
trimmed
1/3 cup cashews
1 1/4 pounds boneless
smoked chicken
breast, cut into slices

Dressing
1/3 cup olive oil
3 tablespoons white
wine vinegar
3 tablespoons sweet
and sour sauce
Few drops Tabasco
sauce

1 On a serving plate
spread a thin layer of
salad sprouts. Top with
remaining ingredients.
2 For dressing, in a
screw-top jar combine
oil, vinegar, sweet and
sour sauce, and Tabasco
sauce. Cover; shake well.
3 Drizzle dressing over
salad just before serving.

Note: A combination of
bean sprouts and alfalfa
sprouts can be used if
salad sprouts are not
available. Ordinary
mushrooms can be
substituted for the
oyster variety.

7

Chicken and Corn Soup

1. For the Chicken and Corn Soup, skim off scum from stock as it boils.

2. Add chopped vegetables, peppercorns, and bouquet garni to the stock.

Chicken and Corn Soup

Preparation time:
  1½ hours
Chilling time:
  Overnight
Cooking time:
  12 minutes
Serves 6

Chicken Stock
3 to 4 pounds chicken
  bones, meat, and
  giblets, trimmed of fat
Cold water
2 onions
2 carrots
2 stalks celery
6 peppercorns
Bouquet garni (see Note)

Soup
3 cups chicken stock
2 cups shredded cooked
  chicken
17-ounce can cream-
  style corn
2 tablespoons cornstarch
2 tablespoons water

6 green onions, chopped
1 tablespoon soy sauce
1 teaspoon sesame oil
Green onions, sliced

1 For stock, in a large
saucepan place chicken
and cold water to cover.
Slowly bring to a boil.
Skim off any scum that
forms during cooking.
2 Coarsely chop
vegetables. Add to
chicken mixture with
peppercorns and
bouquet garni. Simmer,
uncovered, for 1 to
1½ hours, adding more
water, if necessary.
3 Strain stock into a
large bowl, discarding
bones and vegetables.
Cool stock. Cover with
plastic wrap. Chill
overnight; remove any
hardened fat on top.
4 For soup: In a large
saucepan bring 3 cups
stock to a boil; add
chicken and corn. Stir
together cornstarch and
2 tablespoons water;

stir into chicken mixture.
Cook and stir till
thickened. Cook and stir
2 minutes more.
5 Stir in chopped green
onions, soy sauce, and
sesame oil. Simmer for
2 minutes. Garnish with
sliced green onions.

Note: A bouquet garni
consists of a few sprigs
of parsley, a bay leaf,
and 1 teaspoon dried
thyme tied in a double
thickness of cheesecloth.

Chicken Soup with Dumplings

Preparation time:
  25 minutes
Cooking time: 15 minutes
Serves 6

1 boneless skinless
  chicken breast
2 eggs
½ cup finely chopped
  leek

3. Strain simmered stock into a bowl
and discard bones and vegetables.

4. Blend cornstarch and water and stir
into soup. Cook and stir till thickened.

*1/2 cup finely chopped
onion*
*1/2 cup finely chopped
carrot*
2 cups soft bread crumbs
*1 tablespoon chopped
parsley*
1 teaspoon pepper
*1 teaspoon dried thyme,
crushed*
*3 cups homemade
chicken stock or
canned chicken broth*
Chopped parsley

1 Cut chicken into
small pieces. In a food
processor, process eggs.
till thick and creamy.
Add leek, onion, and
carrot and process till
smooth. Add chicken;
process till smooth.
Transfer to a bowl.
2 Stir bread crumbs,
1 tablespoon parsley,
pepper, and thyme into
chicken mixture. Shape
into dumplings using
2 large spoons dipped
in cold water. Place on
a waxed-paper-lined
tray. Cover till all
dumplings are made.
3 In a large saucepan
bring chicken stock to a
boil; reduce heat. Gently
spoon dumplings into
stock. Simmer,
uncovered, till they
float to the surface.
Cover and simmer for
10 minutes more.
4 Divide dumplings
and chicken stock evenly
into 6 soup bowls.
Garnish with parsley.

Chicken Laksa

Preparation time:
  20 minutes
Cooking time:
  25 minutes
Serves 4

*4 cups homemade
chicken stock or
canned chicken broth*
*1 pound boneless
skinless chicken
breasts, cut into strips*
4 ounces bean sprouts
*4 ounces cellophane or
other dried noodles*
2 tablespoons cooking oil
1 onion, finely chopped
1 clove garlic, crushed
2 fresh chilies, chopped
*2 teaspoons ground
coriander*
*1 teaspoon ground
turmeric*
2 cups milk
1 cup coconut milk
2 green onions, sliced

1 In large saucepan
bring chicken stock to a
boil; reduce heat. Add
chicken. Simmer for
5 minutes. Remove
saucepan from heat,
cover, stand 10 minutes.
2 Remove chicken
from saucepan with a
slotted spoon, reserving
stock. Set aside.
3 Blanch sprouts by
placing in boiling water
for 30 seconds. Drain;
rinse with cold water;
drain. Set aside.

4 Place cellophane
noodles in bowl. Cover
with boiling water. Let
stand 10 minutes.
Drain. Set aside.
5 In a saucepan heat
oil. Cook onion and
garlic in oil till tender.
Add chilies, coriander,
and turmeric. Cook and
stir for 30 seconds.
Gradually add milk and
coconut milk. Simmer,
uncovered, 15 minutes,
stirring occasionally.
6 Divide cellophane
noodles between 4 soup
bowls. Top with equal
portions of sprouts and
chicken. Pour soup over
chicken mixture.
Garnish with sliced
green onions.

Herb-Marinated
Chicken Wings

Preparation time:
  35 minutes
Marinating time:
  Overnight
Cooking time:
  35 minutes
Makes about 24

2 pounds chicken wings
*2 teaspoons finely
shredded lemon peel*
1 tablespoon lemon juice
1/2 cup olive oil
*2 tablespoons dry white
wine*
*2 tablespoons white
wine vinegar*

Chicken Laksa and Chicken Soup with Dumplings (page 9)

Clockwise from top: Chicken San Choy Bow (page 14), Herb-Marinated Chicken Wings (page 10), Warm Chicken-Bell Pepper Salad

3 cloves garlic, crushed
1 tablespoon chopped parsley
1 tablespoon chopped fresh dill
Freshly ground pepper

1 Rinse chicken and pat dry with paper towels. Cut off wing tips at joint. Cut wings in half through center joint.
2 Holding one end of each wing half, trim around bone with a sharp knife to free meat. (Discard small bone visible in smaller half of wing.) Cut, scrape, and pull meat down to the large end. Pull skin and meat down over end of bone to resemble drumsticks.
3 For marinade, in a large bowl combine all remaining ingredients. Add chicken. Cover; marinate overnight.
4 Drain chicken, reserving marinade. Arrange chicken on a baking sheet; bake in a 350° oven 30 to 35 minutes, brushing occasionally with reserved marinade.

HINT
Homemade chicken stock will keep for one week in the refrigerator or four months in the freezer.

Warm Chicken-Bell Pepper Salad

Preparation time:
  35 minutes
Cooking time:
  None
Serves 4

2¹/₂- to 3-pound whole cooked chicken
2 tablespoons olive oil
1 small onion, sliced
2 large bell peppers, cut into strips
1 tablespoon soy sauce
¹/₄ teaspoon five-spice powder
Pinch sugar
Freshly ground pepper
1 tablespoon vinegar
¹/₃ cup blanched almonds, toasted

1 Remove skin and meat from chicken; discard skin. Set chicken aside. In a saucepan heat 1 tablespoon of the oil. Cook onion in oil till tender. Add bell pepper and cook 5 minutes or till crisp-tender.
2 Add cooked chicken, soy sauce, five-spice powder, and sugar to bell pepper mixture. Season with pepper. Heat through. Transfer to a serving bowl.
3 In a small bowl combine vinegar and remaining 1 tablespoon oil. Drizzle over chicken. Sprinkle with almonds.

13

Chicken San Choy Bow

Preparation time:
  20 minutes
Cooking time:
  8 minutes
Serves 6

1 pound ground
  chicken
4 ounces sliced ham,
  finely chopped
1 egg
1 tablespoon soy sauce
1 teaspoon cornstarch
1 tablespoon cooking oil
6-ounce can chopped
  mushrooms, drained
1/4 cup chopped
  bamboo shoots
1 onion, finely chopped
1 teaspoon finely
  chopped gingerroot
Lettuce leaves

1 In a bowl combine chicken and ham. Whisk together egg, soy sauce, and cornstarch till well combined. Stir into chicken mixture.
2 Heat a large skillet or wok over high heat. Add oil. Stir-fry chicken mixture for 2 to 3 minutes or till chicken is no longer pink, breaking up any lumps with a fork. Add mushrooms, bamboo shoots, onion, and gingerroot. Stir-fry for 2 minutes more.
3 To serve, spoon chicken mixture onto lettuce leaves. Roll up leaves and serve with plum sauce.

Note: This dish is served as a first course, and eaten with the fingers.

Chicken Liver and Brandy Pâté

Preparation time:
  10 minutes
Cooking time:
  15 minutes
Makes about 1 1/2 cups

1/4 cup butter
1 large onion, chopped
2 cloves garlic, crushed
2 slices bacon, chopped
8 ounces chicken livers,
  trimmed
2 tablespoons whipping
  cream
1 tablespoon brandy
1/4 teaspoon dried
  thyme, crushed
Freshly ground pepper

Topping
1/4 cup butter or
  margarine, melted
Fresh thyme

1 In a saucepan melt 1/4 cup butter. Cook onion, garlic, and bacon in butter till onion is tender and bacon is done.
2 Add chicken livers to pan. Cook, stirring occasionally for 5 to 10 minutes or till no longer pink. Stir in whipping cream, brandy, and dried thyme.
3 Transfer mixture to a food processor. Cover and process till smooth. Season with pepper. Pour into serving dishes.

Chicken Liver and Brandy Pâté

14

4 For topping, pour ¼ cup melted butter or margarine over the top of pâté. Garnish with fresh thyme. Refrigerate several hours or overnight. Serve with crackers, toast, or crusty French bread.

Note: Pâté will keep in the refrigerator for up to one week, covered with plastic wrap. Most pâtés are at their best one or two days after they are made.

Chicken and Mushroom Terrine

Preparation time:
  35 minutes
Cooking time:
  1 hour
Makes 1 loaf (16 slices)

4 *ounces mushrooms*
1 *pound boneless skinless chicken breasts, finely chopped*
8 *ounces chicken livers, trimmed*
2 *slices bacon*
2 *eggs*
½ *cup light cream*
1 *tablespoon chopped fresh basil*
Freshly ground pepper
6 *slices bacon*

1 Place mushrooms in a food processor or blender. Cover and

Chicken and Mushroom Terrine

process till finely chopped. Set aside.
2 In food processor or blender place chicken, chicken livers, and bacon. Cover and process till well combined. Add eggs, one at a time, processing well after each addition.
3 With machine running, slowly pour in cream and process till smooth. Transfer to a bowl. Stir in mushrooms and basil. Season with pepper.
4 Line the bottom and sides of 9 x 5 x 3-inch loaf pan with bacon. Pour chicken mixture into loaf pan. Fold ends of bacon over to cover top.

5 Place loaf pan in a roasting pan. Fill halfway with boiling water (see Note). Bake in a 350° oven for 1 hour or till firm. Drain off excess fat. Cool. Refrigerate till cold and ready to serve.
6 To serve, unmold onto a serving platter. Slice and serve with French bread or salad greens.

Note: This method of cooking is known as bain marie. It protects delicate mixtures from becoming overcooked and tough during long periods of cooking.

Family Favorites

The aroma of a slow-cooking roast or a succulent chicken pie gets the tastebuds working in anticipation of a good meal. The exertions of the working week are soon alleviated when family members gather around the table to chat unhurriedly and savor a beautifully cooked and well-flavored meal. Traditional recipes such as Roast Chicken with Parsley Stuffing are hard to beat. And we've drawn on some international influences – from India, South East Asia, Italy, and France – to bring your family food at its best. These dishes require a little more preparation and cooking time than weekdays may allow, so keep them in mind for weekends and special occasion dinners.

Deep-Dish Chicken Pie

Preparation time:
  30 minutes
Cooking time:
  25 minutes
Serves 4

1/4 cup butter
1 small onion, chopped
4 ounces mushrooms, halved
1/2 cup finely chopped celery
1/4 cup all-purpose flour
1 1/2 cups homemade chicken stock or canned chicken broth

2 cups chopped cooked chicken
1/2 cup light cream
Freshly ground pepper
1/2 x 17 1/4-ounce package frozen puff pastry, thawed
1 beaten egg

1 In a saucepan melt butter. Add onion and cook till tender. Add mushrooms and celery; cook and stir for 3 to 4 minutes.
2 Stir in flour. Add chicken stock. Cook and stir till thickened. Cook and stir 1 minute more. Stir in chicken and cream. Season with pepper.

Clockwise from top: Deep-Dish Chicken Pie, Roast Chicken with Bacon and Bread Sauce (page 18), Spanish-Style Chicken Casserole (page 22)

3 Spoon mixture into a greased deep 6-cup casserole or soufflé dish. Cut pastry to fit the dish and place over chicken mixture. Decorate with pastry leaves or other shapes. Brush with beaten egg.
4 Bake, uncovered, in a 400° oven for 20 to 25 minutes or till pastry is golden brown.

Roast Chicken with Bacon and Bread Sauce

Preparation time:
  45 minutes
Cooking time:
  1¹/2 hours
Serves 4

2¹/2 to 3-pound whole chicken
2 large sprigs fresh rosemary
2 cloves garlic, peeled
1 tablespoon butter or margarine, melted
3 slices bacon
¹/2 cup chicken stock or canned broth

Bread Sauce
1 small onion, finely chopped
1 cup milk
4 peppercorns
1 bay leaf
1 cup soft bread crumbs
1 tablespoon butter or margarine

Pinch ground cloves
2 teaspoons fresh rosemary leaves

1 Rinse chicken and pat dry with paper towels. Place rosemary sprigs, garlic, and 1 tablespoon butter or margarine inside cavity of chicken.
2 Criss-cross bacon over chicken breast. Secure bacon in several spots with toothpicks.
3 Place chicken on a rack in a roasting pan. Pour stock in pan. Bake, uncovered, in a 350° oven 1¹/2 hours or till tender and no longer pink, basting frequently with chicken stock. (If necessary, cover chicken with foil to prevent bacon from overbrowning.) Let stand 15 minutes.
4 For sauce, in a small saucepan combine onion, milk, peppercorns, and bay leaf. Simmer for 15 minutes. Strain. Stir in bread crumbs,

1 tablespoon butter or margarine, and cloves.
5 Add 2 teaspoons rosemary to the pan juices from chicken. Carve the chicken and pour pan juices over the top. Serve with sauce.

Coq au Vin

This popular dish is a tradition in French Provincial cooking.

Preparation time:
  30 minutes
Cooking time:
  1 hour
Serves 4 to 6

2 teaspoons cooking oil
1 large onion, chopped
10 chicken thighs, skinned
2 cloves garlic, crushed
4 ounces ham, chopped
8 ounces small mushrooms

HINT
If you are buying frozen chicken to store in your freezer at home, make it the last item to put in your shopping cart and transport it home as soon as possible. If it is still frozen solid when you get home, put it right into your freezer without rewrapping it. If it has started to thaw, place it in the refrigerator and allow it to thaw completely. Then cook it, cool it, place in a freezer container or wrap, and freeze. Do not thaw and then refreeze uncooked or cooked poultry because this decreases the quality and flavor of the meat.

Coq au Vin

2 cups dry red wine
2 tablespoons cornstarch
2 tablespoons water
2 tablespoons chopped
  parsley

1 In a large skillet heat oil. Cook onion in hot oil till tender. Add chicken and garlic. Lightly brown chicken on all sides. Remove chicken from skillet. Set aside.
2 In same skillet add ham and mushrooms to onion mixture. Cook and stir for 1 minute. Return chicken to skillet. Add red wine. Bring to a boil; reduce heat. Cover and simmer

for 1 hour or till chicken is tender and no longer pink.
3 Stir together cornstarch and water till smooth. Add to wine mixture. Cook and stir till thickened and bubbly. Cook and stir 2 minutes more.
4 Add parsley just before serving. Serve with hot cooked rice, salad, and crusty bread.

Note: This dish can be made up to two days in advance and refrigerated till serving time. This allows the flavors to develop beautifully.

Almond-Crusted Chicken

Preparation time:
  30 minutes
Cooking time:
  45 minutes
Serves 4

2¹/2- to 3-pound whole
  chicken
1 egg, lightly beaten
2 cups shredded Swiss
  cheese
¹/2 cup chopped slivered
  almonds
¹/4 cup grated Parmesan
  cheese
¹/4 teaspoon paprika
Fresh basil

19

1 Rinse chicken and pat dry with paper towels. Cut up chicken. Dip chicken pieces in egg. Drain off excess.
2 In a bowl combine Swiss cheese, almonds, Parmesan cheese, and paprika. Coat chicken pieces in almond mixture. Place chicken in a lightly greased shallow baking pan.
3 Bake in a 400° oven for 45 minutes or till chicken is tender and no longer pink. Garnish with fresh basil.

Note: It is important to make sure chicken is thoroughly cooked before eating. Insert a skewer into the thickest part of the chicken. If the juices run clear and the meat next to the bone is no longer pink, the chicken is done. If the juices or meat are pink, continue cooking.

Chicken Parmigiana with Tomato Sauce

Preparation time:
   40 minutes
Cooking time:
   12 minutes
Serves 4

Tomato Sauce
1 tablespoon olive oil
1 onion, finely chopped
14 1/2-ounce can
   chopped tomatoes
1/4 cup dry red wine
3 tablespoons tomato
   paste
1 clove garlic, crushed
1/2 teaspoon dried
   oregano, crushed
Freshly ground pepper

Chicken Parmigiana
1 egg
2 tablespoons milk
3/4 cup dry bread crumbs
1/2 cup grated Parmesan
   cheese

1. For Almond-Crusted Chicken, cut legs and thighs from bird in one whole piece.

2. Cut off wings. Leave a small piece of meat from breast attached.

Almond-crusted Chicken

3. *Cut through rib bones along each side, near backbone, and remove breast meat.*

4. *Coat pieces in beaten egg, then in almond mixture.*

21

4 boneless skinless
chicken breasts,
pounded thin
1/4 cup olive oil

1 For sauce, cook
onion in hot oil till
tender. Stir in undrained
tomatoes, wine, tomato
paste, garlic, and
oregano. Season with
pepper. Bring to a boil;
reduce heat. Simmer,
uncovered, 15 minutes.
2 In a shallow dish
combine egg and milk.
In another shallow dish
combine bread crumbs
and 1/4 cup of the
Parmesan cheese. Dip
chicken in egg mixture
and coat with bread
crumb mixture.
Refrigerate 5 minutes.
3 Heat 2 tablespoons
of the oil in a large
skillet. Cook 2 breasts
at a time in hot oil till
brown and tender.
Repeat with remaining
oil and chicken. Drain
on paper towels.
4 To serve, top chicken
with tomato sauce and
sprinkle with remaining
1/4 cup Parmesan cheese.

> **HINT**
> After cooking a
> casserole ahead, cool
> it rapidly by
> immersing the base
> of the dish in ice
> water. Then store it,
> covered, in the
> refrigerator.

Spanish-Style Chicken Casserole

Preparation time:
  20 minutes
Cooking time:
  35 to 45 minutes
Serves 8

2 tablespoons cooking
  oil
4 pounds chicken pieces
Freshly ground pepper
2 onions, chopped
2 red or green bell
  peppers, cut into strips
6 slices prosciutto,
  chopped
2 cloves garlic, crushed
14 1/2-ounce can
  chopped tomatoes
1/2 cup dry white wine
12 pitted ripe olives
12 pitted green olives

1 In a large skillet heat
oil. Cook chicken, a few
pieces at a time,
till brown. Season
with pepper. Transfer
to plate.
2 In same saucepan
cook onions, bell
peppers, prosciutto, and
garlic till onion is
tender but not brown.
Add chicken, undrained
tomatoes, wine, and
olives.
3 Bring to a boil;
reduce heat. Simmer,
uncovered, for 35 to
45 minutes or till
chicken is tender and no
longer pink.

Chicken Stroganoff

Preparation time:
  20 minutes
Cooking time:
  15 minutes
Serves 6

2 tablespoons butter
2 tablespoons cooking
  oil
2 onions, thinly sliced
2 cloves garlic, crushed
8 boneless skinless
  chicken thighs, sliced
8 ounces mushrooms,
  sliced
2 teaspoons paprika
1 cup sour cream
1/4 cup tomato paste
1 tablespoon
  all-purpose flour
Freshly ground pepper
2 tablespoons chopped
  parsley

1 In a large skillet heat
butter and oil. Cook
onion and garlic in oil
mixture till onion is
tender. Add chicken.
Cook for 5 minutes.
Add mushrooms and
paprika. Cook and stir
till chicken is tender.
2 Stir together sour
cream, tomato paste,
and flour. Add to skillet.
Cook over low heat till
heated through. Season
with pepper and garnish
with chopped parsley.
Serve with hot rice,
pasta, or egg noodles.

Chicken Stroganoff

Chicken Loaf in Sour Cream Pastry

Preparation time:
  45 minutes
Chilling time:
  1 hour
Cooking time:
  45 minutes
Serves 6

Pastry
2¹/2 cups all-purpose flour
1 cup butter, cut into
  small pieces
¹/4 cup sour cream
1 egg yolk

Filling
¹/4 cup butter
1¹/2 pounds ground
  chicken
1 large onion, chopped
¹/2 cup homemade
  chicken stock or
  canned broth
4 ounces mushrooms,
  finely chopped
3 tablespoons finely
  chopped chives
2 tablespoons fresh
  rosemary leaves
Freshly ground pepper
¹/2 cup soft bread crumbs
2 eggs, beaten
³/4 cup shredded
  cheddar cheese

¹/4 cup chopped parsley
1 egg, lightly beaten

1 For pastry, place
flour in a bowl. Cut in
1 cup butter with a
pastry blender till
mixture resembles fine
crumbs. Combine sour
cream and egg yolk;
add to flour. Stir till a
firm dough forms.
Gently knead till
smooth. Wrap in plastic
wrap and chill for at
least 1 hour.
2 For filling, in a large
saucepan melt ¹/4 cup
butter. Add chicken and

23

Chicken Loaf in Sour Cream Pastry

onion and cook till chicken is no longer pink, breaking up any lumps. Add chicken stock, mushrooms, chives, and rosemary. Season with pepper. Bring to a boil; reduce heat. Simmer, uncovered, 20 minutes or till all liquid is absorbed. Stir in bread crumbs; cool.
3 In a bowl combine 2 eggs, shredded

cheese, and parsley. Stir into chicken mixture.
4 On a lightly floured surface roll out half of the pastry large enough to line bottom and sides of a 11 x 7 x 1 1/2-inch baking pan, leaving some dough to hang over edge. Spoon filling evenly over pastry. Brush edges with 1 beaten egg.
5 On a lightly floured surface roll out three-

quarters of remaining pastry to cover filling. Trim and press edges together to seal. Brush with remaining beaten egg. Roll remaining pastry into a rectangle; cut into lengthwise strips.
6 Lay pastry strips in a criss-cross pattern on top of pastry. Brush with egg; pierce top to let the steam escape.
7 Bake in a 350° oven for 40 to 45 minutes or till pastry is golden. Cool slightly before serving. Cut into slices and serve with mushrooms, chives, and yellow cherry tomatoes.

Curried Yogurt Chicken

Preparation time:
  20 minutes
Marinating time:
  Several hours
Cooking time:
  45 minutes
Serves 6

1 cup plain yogurt
1/2 cup cream of coconut
1/4 cup fresh coriander or cilantro, chopped
1 onion, finely chopped
1 clove garlic, crushed
1 teaspoon finely shredded lime peel

HINT
Coat chicken pieces for pan-frying in flour seasoned with your favorite herbs or spices. Or, dip the pieces of chicken in beaten egg and coat with soft or fine dry bread crumbs mixed with grated cheese, chopped nuts, fresh herbs, spices, or a combination of these. Press the coating on firmly. If using nuts, cook the chicken over a low or medium-low heat to prevent the nuts from burning and becoming bitter.

Curried Yoghurt Chicken

1 tablespoon lime juice
1 tablespoon curry
  powder
Freshly ground pepper
2 pounds chicken
  pieces
1 cup plain yogurt,
  extra

1 In a large shallow
glass or ceramic dish
combine 1 cup yogurt,
cream of coconut,
coriander or cilantro,
onion, garlic, lime peel,
lime juice, and curry
powder. Season with
pepper. Add the
chicken pieces, stirring

till well coated.
2 Cover dish with
plastic wrap. Marinate
in the refrigerator
several hours or
overnight to allow
flavor to develop.
3 Remove chicken
from marinade. Place
in a shallow baking
pan. Bake in a 350°
oven for 45 minutes or
till chicken is tender
and no longer pink.
Serve with 1 cup
yogurt and garnish
with fresh coriander or
cilantro. Accompany
with boiled rice.

Chicken Chop Suey

Preparation time:
  20 minutes
Cooking time:
  8 minutes
Serves 6

2 tablespoons cooking
  oil
12 ounces boneless
  skinless chicken
  breasts, thinly sliced
8 ounces lean ground
  pork
1/2 small Chinese
  cabbage, shredded

25

Chicken Chop Suey

1. For *Chicken Chop Suey*, stir-fry sliced chicken and ground pork in hot oil.

2. *Stir-fry chopped vegetables and garlic for 3 minutes or till crisp-tender.*

4 stalks celery, sliced
2 carrots, chopped
1 onion, chopped
1 red or green bell
   pepper, chopped
1 clove garlic, crushed
1 cup chicken stock or
   canned broth
1 tablespoon soy sauce
2 teaspoons cornstarch
1 teaspoon ground
   ginger
8-ounce can bamboo
   shoots, drained
8-ounce can sliced water
   chestnuts, drained
1 6-ounce jar whole
   small mushrooms,
   drained

1 Heat a large wok or
skillet over high heat.
Add oil. Stir-fry chicken
and pork for 3 to 4
minutes or till chicken
is no longer pink and
pork is brown. Remove
meat from skillet.
2 In same skillet add
cabbage, celery,
carrots, onion, bell
pepper, and garlic.

Stir-fry for 3 minutes.
3 Stir together chicken
stock, soy sauce,
cornstarch, and ginger.
Add to skillet. Cook
and stir till thickened
and bubbly. Cook and
stir 2 minutes more.
4 Return chicken and
pork to skillet. Add
bamboo shoots, water
chestnuts, and
mushrooms. Cook and
stir till heated through.
Serve with hot cooked
rice or noodles.

Cabbage Rolls filled with Chicken

Preparation time:
   35 minutes
Cooking time:
   1 hour
Serves 4

Filling
1 tablespoon olive oil
1 onion, finely chopped

12 ounces ground
   chicken
4 ounces mushrooms,
   chopped
Freshly ground pepper
1/2 cup cooked brown
   rice
1 egg white
8 to 10 whole cabbage
   leaves

Sauce
1 1/2 cups tomato purée
1/2 cup water
1/4 cup light sourcream
1 clove garlic, crushed
1/2 teaspoon sugar
Pinch ground oregano

1 For filling, in a skillet
heat oil. Cook onion in
hot oil till tender. Add
ground chicken and
mushrooms. Cook
and stir till chicken is
no longer pink. Drain
off fat. Season with
pepper. Cool.
2 Transfer chicken
mixture to a large bowl.
Stir in rice and egg
white. Set aside.

3. Add the chicken stock mixture to wok
or skillet.

4. Return meat to wok. Add bamboo
shoots, water chestnuts, and mushrooms.

3 Blanch cabbage leaves by placing them in boiling water for 1 to 2 minutes. Rinse with cold water; drain. Remove center veins from cabbage leaves, keeping each leaf in 1 piece.

4 For sauce, in a bowl combine tomato purée, water, sour cream, garlic, sugar, and oregano. Set aside.

5 To assemble, spoon 1 to 2 tablespoons filling (depending on the size of the leaf) on each cabbage leaf. Fold in sides. Starting at an unfolded edge, roll up each leaf, making sure folded sides are included in roll. Secure with toothpicks, if necessary.

6 Place rolls, seam side down, in a baking dish, placing rolls close together. Pour sauce over rolls. Bake in a 350° oven for 1 hour.

Caribbean Chicken Casserole

Preparation time:
  20 minutes
Marinating time:
  30 minutes
Cooking time:
  45 minutes
Serves 4

2¹/₂- to 3-pound
  chicken, cut up
2 teaspoons finely
  shredded lemon peel
2 tablespoons lemon
  juice
1 tablespoon teriyaki
  sauce
Freshly ground pepper
2 tablespoons cooking
  oil
1 onion, sliced
1 clove garlic, crushed
15¹/₂-ounce can crushed
  pineapple
2 large tomatoes, peeled
  and chopped
¹/₃ cup raisins
¹/₄ cup flaked coconut

1 tablespoon chopped
  fresh coriander or
  cilantro
¹/₄ teaspoon ground
  cinnamon
2 tablespoons water
1 tablespoon cornstarch

1 Rinse chicken and pat dry. In a bowl combine chicken, lemon peel, lemon juice, and teriyaki sauce. Season with pepper. Marinate in the refrigerator for 30 minutes, stirring occasionally.

2 In a large skillet heat oil. Drain chicken, reserving marinade. Brown chicken in hot oil on all sides. Transfer to large casserole. Add reserved marinade.

3 In same skillet cook onion and garlic in oil till tender. Add to chicken mixture. Combine undrained pineapple, tomatoes, raisins, coconut, coriander or cilantro,

1. For Cabbage Rolls, blanch cabbage leaves briefly in boiling water.

2. Roll leaves around filling to make neat bundles. Secure with toothpicks.

Roast Chicken with Parsley Stuffing

45 minutes or till chicken is tender and no longer pink. Stir together water and cornstarch. Stir into chicken mixture. Bake, uncovered, for 10 minutes more or till thickened, stirring once. Serve with rice.

Roast Chicken with Parsley Stuffing

Preparation time:
  35 minutes
Cooking time:
  1 1/4 to 1 1/2 hours
Serves 4

2 1/2- to 3-pound whole chicken
1 onion, chopped
1 clove garlic, crushed
2 tablespoons butter
1 cup parsley, chopped
1 cup soft bread crumbs
1 egg, lightly beaten
Freshly ground pepper

1 Rinse chicken and pat dry with paper towels. Set aside. In a small saucepan cook onion and garlic in butter till tender.
2 In a bowl combine parsley and bread crumbs. Stir in onion mixture and egg. Season with pepper. Loosen skin of chicken from breast. Gently push stuffing under skin.
3 Place chicken on a rack in a roasting pan. Pour about 1 cup water in pan. Bake, uncovered, in a 375° oven for 1 1/4 to 1 1/2 hours or till chicken is tender and no longer pink or a meat thermometer registers 180° to 185°. Let stand 15 minutes before carving. Spoon stuffing into a bowl and serve with chicken.

29

Quick, Smart Solutions

Ease of preparation is one of the most important criteria for busy cooks. Chicken pieces – thighs, wings, breasts, and drumsticks – are readily available in your grocer's meat case. Keep a supply on hand in the freezer. Purchase cooked whole chickens to star in a meal when you are really short on time. You can make things even easier for yourself if you have a well-stocked pantry; sesame oil, tomato sauce, spaghetti sauce, soy sauce, relishes, chutney, herbs, spices, nuts, mustard, pita bread, and pizza crusts will lend flexibility to your cooking without having to make another trip to the grocery store.

Chicken Pita Pizzas

Preparation time:
  15 minutes
Cooking time:
  15 minutes
Serves 6

2 x 6- or 8-inch pita bread rounds
1/4 cup tomato preserves or chutney
1/2 cup shredded cooked chicken
4 ounces mushrooms, sliced
1 small red or green bell pepper, cut into strips

Dried oregano or basil
1 cup shredded mozzarella cheese

1 Place pita bread rounds on a baking sheet. Spread tomato preserves or chutney evenly over each piece of pita bread. Top with chicken, mushrooms, and strips of bell pepper. Season with oregano or basil and sprinkle with mozzarella cheese.
2 Bake pizzas, uncovered, in a 400° oven for 15 minutes or till cheese melts and chicken is heated through.

Chicken Pita Pizza, Grilled Chicken Pizzaiola (page 32)

Grilled Chicken Pizzaiola

Preparation time:
  20 minutes
Cooking time:
  10 minutes
Serves 4

1 tablespoon olive oil
1 large onion, finely
  chopped
2 cloves garlic, chopped
14¹/₂-ounce can
  chopped tomatoes
1 teaspoon dried basil,
  crushed
1 teaspoon dried
  oregano, crushed
1 tablespoon drained
  capers
1 pound boneless
  skinless chicken breasts
Olive oil

1 In a saucepan heat
1 tablespoon oil. Cook
onion and garlic in oil
till tender. Add
undrained tomatoes,
basil, and oregano.
Bring to a boil; reduce
heat. Simmer,
uncovered, 5 minutes or
till thickened, stirring
frequently. Stir in
capers; keep warm.
2 Rinse chicken and
pat dry with paper
towels. Lightly brush
with olive oil. Place on
unheated rack of broiler
pan. Broil about 3
inches from heat for
5 minutes on each side

or till tender and no
longer pink.
3 Place chicken on a
serving platter. Pour
tomato mixture over.

Chicken with Walnuts and Blue Cheese

Preparation time:
  15 minutes
Cooking time:
  15 minutes
Serves 4

8 boneless skinless
  chicken thighs
Olive oil
3 medium tomatoes,
  thickly sliced
¹/₃ cup walnut pieces
6 green onions, finely
  chopped
3 ounces blue cheese,
  crumbled

1 Brush chicken lightly
with olive oil. Place on
unheated rack of broiler
pan. Broil 3 inches from
heat 3 minutes each side
or till almost done.
2 Scatter tomatoes in
an ovenproof dish. Broil
2 minutes. Add chicken.
Sprinkle with walnuts,
green onions, and blue
cheese.
3 Place dish under
broiler and broil about
5 minutes more or till
chicken is tender and
cheese is melted.

Oriental Chicken Kabobs

Preparation time:
  30 minutes
Marinating time:
  30 minutes
Cooking time:
  6 to 8 minutes
Serves 4

1 tablespoon light soy
  sauce
1 tablespoon white wine

Oriental Chicken Kabobs

2 teaspoons whole
  grain mustard
2 teaspoons snipped
  chives
1 teaspoon cooking oil
2 cloves garlic, crushed
1 teaspoon grated
  gingerroot
1 pound boneless
  skinless chicken
  breasts, cut into
  chunks
12 small mushrooms
12 cherry tomatoes
1 onion, cut into 8
  wedges

1 green bell pepper, cut
  into cubes
8-ounce can juice pack
  pineapple rings,
  drained and quartered

1 In a glass bowl
combine soy sauce,
wine, mustard, chives,
oil, garlic, and
gingerroot. Add chicken.
Marinate for 30 minutes
in the refrigerator, stirring
chicken frequently.
2 Drain chicken,
reserving marinade.

Alternately thread
chicken, mushrooms,
tomatoes, onion, bell
pepper, and pineapple
onto skewers.
3 Place skewers on
unheated rack of a
broiler pan. Broil 3 to 4
inches from the heat for
3 to 4 minutes or till
lightly browned. Turn
and brush with reserved
marinade. Broil for
3 to 4 minutes more
or till chicken is tender
and no longer pink.

33

1. For Chicken with Lemon and Coriander, dust chicken pieces with seasoned flour.

2. After browning chicken, add stock, lemon juice, coriander, and garlic to skillet.

Chicken with Lemon and Coriander

Chicken with Lemon and Coriander

Preparation time:
  25 minutes
Cooking time:
  50 minutes
Serves 4

2¹/₂ to 3-pound whole
  chicken, quartered
3 tablespoons
  all-purpose flour
Freshly ground pepper
2 tablespoons olive oil
¹/₂ cup chicken stock or
  canned broth
2 tablespoons lemon juice
2 tablespoons chopped
  fresh coriander or
  cilantro
2 cloves garlic, crushed
1 tablespoon whipping
  cream

1 Rinse chicken; pat dry with paper towels. Coat chicken in flour seasoned with pepper.
2 In a large skillet heat oil over medium-high heat. Brown chicken on all sides. Reduce heat. Add stock, lemon juice, cilantro, and garlic. Cover, simmer 45 minutes or till chicken is tender.
3 Remove chicken from skillet; keep warm. Stir cream into skillet with stock mixture. Bring to a boil. Cook and stir till slightly thickened. Serve over chicken; garnish with lemon wedges.

Chicken Chili Pasta

Preparation time:
  20 minutes
Cooking time:
  25 minutes
Serves 6

2 teaspoons olive oil
1 onion, chopped
1 red or green bell
  pepper, chopped

3. *Remove cooked chicken from skillet and stir cream into pan juices.*

4. *Bring cream mixture to a boil and cook till slightly thickened.*

1 clove garlic, crushed
1 teaspoon chopped
   fresh chili
1 teaspoon chili sauce
1 pound ground
   chicken
14$^{1}/_{2}$-ounce can
   chopped tomatoes
1 cup dry white wine
   or water
$^{1}/_{2}$ teaspoon dried
   oregano, crushed
$^{1}/_{2}$ teaspoon dried basil,
   crushed
Freshly ground pepper
1 pound desired pasta
2 tablespoons chopped
   parsley
Grated Parmesan
   cheese

1 In a large saucepan heat oil. Add onion, bell pepper, and garlic and cook till tender. Stir in chili and chili sauce.
2 Add ground chicken. Cook and stir till no longer pink, breaking up any lumps. Stir in undrained tomatoes, wine or water, oregano, and basil. Season with pepper.
3 Bring to a boil; reduce heat. Simmer, uncovered, for 15 minutes, stirring occasionally.
4 Meanwhile, cook pasta according to package directions or till al dente. Drain. Stir parsley into sauce. Serve sauce over pasta and sprinkle with Parmesan cheese.

Marinated Taco Chicken

Marinated Taco Chicken

Preparation time:
   15 minutes
Marinating time:
   30 minutes
Cooking time:
   15 minutes
Serves 6

$^{2}/_{3}$ cup bottled chunky
   medium taco sauce
$^{1}/_{4}$ cup Dijon mustard
2 tablespoons lemon
   juice
6 boneless skinless
   chicken breasts
2 tablespoons butter

1 In a shallow glass bowl combine taco sauce, mustard, and lemon juice. Add chicken, turning to coat. Marinate chicken in the refrigerator for 30 minutes, turning occasionally.
2 Drain chicken, reserving marinade. In a large skillet melt butter over medium-high heat. Cook chicken about 3 minutes on each side or till chicken is brown.
3 Add reserved marinade to skillet. Bring to a boil; reduce heat. Simmer, uncovered, 5 minutes or till chicken is tender.
4 Remove chicken from skillet with a slotted spoon; keep warm. Simmer liquid in skillet about 5 minutes more till desired consistency. Serve over chicken. Serve with a green salad and tortilla chips.

Chili Tomato Chicken

Preparation time:
  15 minutes
Cooking time:
  10 minutes
Serves 6

2 tablespoons butter or
  margarine
2 tablespoons cooking
  oil
6 boneless skinless
  chicken breasts
1 avocado, peeled,
  pitted, and sliced

3 tomatoes, thickly
  sliced
2 cups shredded
  Monterey Jack cheese

Chili Sauce
1 clove garlic, crushed
1 cup tomato purée
1 tablespoon chili
  sauce
1 teaspoon chopped
  fresh chili
1 teaspoon brown
  sugar
1/4 teaspoon dried
  oregano, crushed
Few drops Tabasco
  sauce
Freshly ground pepper

1 In a large skillet heat butter or margarine and oil over medium heat. Add chicken and cook for 5 minutes on each side or till tender and no longer pink. Transfer to shallow ovenproof dish.
2 Top chicken with avocado slices, tomato slices and cheese. Bake in 350° oven 5 minutes or till cheese melts.
3 Meanwhile, for sauce, remove all but 1 teaspoon fat from skillet. Cook garlic in skillet till tender. Stir in

Chilli Tomato Chicken

Tuscan Chicken

tomato purée, chili sauce, fresh chili, brown sugar, oregano, and Tabasco sauce. Season with pepper. Bring to a boil; reduce heat. Simmer, uncovered, for 3 to 5 minutes or till desired consistency. Serve with chicken.

HINT

Fresh chicken has a pleasant, very mild and fresh aroma. Do not buy chicken with an unpleasant aroma or appearance. Make sure the package is not open.

Tuscan Chicken

Preparation time:
  20 minutes
Cooking time:
  15 minutes
Serves 4

1/4 *cup butter*
1 *pound boneless skinless chicken breasts, cut into* 3/4-*inch cubes*
2 *tablespoons brandy*
8 *ounces cherry tomatoes*
8 *ounces mushrooms, sliced*
1 *cup dry white wine or chicken broth*

Freshly ground pepper
Dried rosemary, crushed

1 In a large skillet melt butter over medium heat. Add chicken; cook and stir for 3 minutes.
2 Add brandy, tomatoes, and mushrooms. Cook and stir for 3 minutes. Add wine or broth and rosemary. Season with pepper.
3 Bring to a boil; reduce heat. Simmer, uncovered, until liquid is reduced and chicken is tender. Serve with steamed zucchini sticks and garnish with fresh rosemary.

Stir-Fried Chicken with Pineapple

Stir-Fried Chicken with Pineapple

Preparation time:
  15 minutes
Cooking time:
  10 minutes
Serves 4

2 tablespoons butter or
½ cup whole or
  slivered almonds
1 tablespoon cooking oil
1 pound boneless
  skinless chicken
  breasts, sliced
1 red bell pepper, sliced
14-ounce can pineapple
  tidbits

2 stalks celery, sliced
1 tablespoon chopped
  fresh mint
2 tablespoons orange
  marmalade

1 In a wok or large skillet melt butter. Cook almonds in butter till light brown. Remove from wok.
2 Add oil to wok or skillet. Stir-fry chicken over high heat for 3 to 4 minutes or till tender and no longer pink. Stir in bell pepper, undrained pineapple, celery, and mint.
3 Add marmalade to wok or skillet. Cook and stir till heated through. Sprinkle with almonds before serving.

HINT
Store raw chicken in the coldest part of your refrigerator and cook within two days of purchase. Whole chickens should be removed from their wrappings, rinsed, patted dry, cut into pieces (if desired), and rewrapped in clean plastic wrap.

39

Chicken Broccoli au Gratin

Chicken Broccoli au Gratin

Preparation time:
  15 minutes
Cooking time:
  30 minutes
Serves 6

2¹/2- to 3-pound
  chicken, cooked and
  cooled (or use a
  purchased barbecued
  chicken)
8 ounces broccoli, cut
  into flowerets
10³/4-ounce can condensed
  cream of chicken soup
1 cup sour cream
¹/2 cup milk
4 green onions, sliced
1 teaspoon curry
  powder
Freshly ground
  pepper
¹/4 cup shredded
  cheddar cheese
¹/4 teaspoon paprika

1 Remove chicken
meat from bone,
remove skin and cut
into large pieces. Set
aside.
2 Cook broccoli in
boiling water for 1 to
2 minutes. Drain in a
colander and rinse with
cold water. Drain.
Place in a greased
2-quart casserole dish.
Top with chicken
pieces.
3 In a bowl stir
together soup, sour
cream, milk, green
onions, and curry
powder. Season with
pepper. Spoon over
chicken mixture.
Sprinkle with cheese
and paprika.
4 Bake, uncovered, in
a 350° oven for 30 to
40 minutes or till
golden brown. Serve
with hot cooked rice.

Teriyaki Kabobs

Preparation time:
  20 minutes
Marinating time:
  1 hour
Cooking time:
  8 to 10 minutes
Serves 4

1/4 cup soy sauce
1/4 cup cooking oil
1/4 cup dry sherry
2 cloves garlic, crushed
2 tablespoons brown
  sugar
2 teaspoons finely
  shredded orange peel
2 teaspoons grated
  gingerroot
1 pound boneless skinless
  chicken breasts, in
  1-inch cubes

1 Combine soy sauce,
oil, sherry, garlic,
brown sugar, orange
peel, and gingerroot.
Add chicken, tossing to
coat. Cover and
marinate in refrigerator.
2 Drain chicken,
reserving marinade.
Thread chicken onto
metal skewers or bamboo
skewers that have been
soaked in water.
3 Grill kabobs on an
uncovered grill over
medium-hot coals
8 to 10 minutes or till
chicken is tender,
turning once and
brushing with reserved
marinade.

Tarragon Lemon Chicken

Choose your favorite
combination of herbs
and spices for this
recipe.
Preparation time:
  20 minutes
Cooking time:
  15 to 20 minutes
Serves 4

1/3 cup butter or
  margarine
2 tablespoons finely
  chopped chives
1 tablespoon finely
  chopped fresh cilantro
1 tablespoon lemon
  juice
1/2 teaspoon dried
  tarragon, crushed
1/4 teaspoon paprika
1 pound boneless
  skinless chicken thighs
Freshly ground pepper

1 Place butter or
margarine in a small
saucepan over low heat,
stirring till melted. Add
chives, cilantro, lemon
juice, tarragon, and
paprika.
2 Season chicken with
pepper. Grill on an
uncovered grill directly
over medium coals for
15 to 20 minutes or till
chicken is tender and no
longer pink, turning
once and brushing with
butter mixture often.
Serve hot or cold.

Marinated Wings

Preparation time:
  20 minutes
Marinating time:
  Overnight
Cooking time:
  30 minutes
Serves 6

1 onion, finely chopped
1/4 cup sour cream
2 tablespoons cooking
  oil
1 teaspoon finely
  shredded lemon peel
2 tablespoons lemon
  juice
1 tablespoon honey
1 tablespoon soy sauce
1 teaspoon dried basil,
  crushed
Freshly ground pepper
2 pounds chicken wings

1 In a shallow glass or
ceramic dish combine
onion, sour cream, oil,
lemon peel, lemon juice,
honey, soy sauce, and
basil. Season with
pepper. Add chicken,
stirring to coat. Cover
and marinate in the
refrigerator overnight.
2 Drain chicken,
reserving marinade.
Grill chicken over
medium coals for
15 to 20 minutes,
turning occasionally.
Brush with reserved
marinade and cook
10 minutes more or till
chicken is tender.

Barbecued Chicken Burgers

Barbecued Chicken Burgers

Preparation time:
  30 minutes
Cooking time:
  15 minutes
Serves 4

12 ounces ground
  chicken
4 green onions, finely
  chopped

¹/2 cup soft bread
  crumbs
¹/4 teaspoon dried basil,
  crushed
2 tablespoons cooking
  oil
Lettuce leaves
Hamburger buns
4 slices bacon, cooked
  crisp
1 avocado, peeled,
  pitted, and sliced

1 In a bowl combine
chicken, onions, bread
crumbs, and basil.

Shape into 4 patties.
2 Brush grill rack with
oil. Grill burgers on an
uncovered grill directly
over medium-hot coals
about 15 minutes or
till no longer pink,
turning once.
3 Serve burgers on
toasted lettuce-lined
hamburger buns with
bacon and avocado, or
other vegetables such as
shredded carrot or
zucchini, or sautéed
mushrooms.

45

Cornish Hens with Lemon, Sesame, and Coriander,
Oriental Chicken (page 48)

1. For Cornish game hens, use sharp
kitchen scissors to cut away the backbone.

2. Press firmly and flatten hens prior to
marinating.

Cornish Hens with Lemon, Sesame, and Coriander

Preparation time:
  20 minutes
Marinating time:
  Overnight
Cooking time:
  30 minutes
Serves 6

3 frozen cornish game
  hens, thawed
1/2 cup lemon juice
2 tablespoons olive oil
1 tablespoon coriander
  seeds, crushed
2 cloves garlic, crushed
2 teaspoons sesame oil
Shredded lemon peel
Lemon slices

1 Rinse hens and pat dry with paper towels. Using kitchen shears, cut along one side of the backbone. Then cut along the other side and discard backbone.

Flatten each hen slightly. Place in shallow glass or ceramic dish.
2 Combine lemon juice, olive oil, coriander seeds, garlic, and sesame oil. Pour over hens in dish, Cover and marinate in the refrigerator overnight, turning occasionally.
3 Drain hens, reserving marinade. Grill hens directly over medium coals for 20 to 30 minutes or till no longer pink, turning and brushing with reserved marinade occasionally. Serve hot or cold, garnished with lemon peel and lemon slices.

HINT
Cornish game hens are special hybrid birds about 4 or 5 weeks old and weighing 1 to 11/2 pounds. Allow about 1/2 bird per serving.

3. Crush coriander seeds and add to oils, lemon juice, and garlic.

4. Place hens in a glass baking dish and pour marinade over them.

Deviled Chicken

Preparation time:
  25 minutes
Marinating time:
  1 hour
Cooking time:
  25 to 30 minutes
Serves 4

1 tomato, peeled and
  finely chopped
1/2 cup tomato sauce
2 tablespoons dry red
  wine
1 tablespoon olive oil
1 tablespoon tomato
  paste
2 teaspoons
  Worcestershire sauce
1/4 teaspoon dried
  Italian seasoning,
  crushed
Few drops Tabasco sauce
4 chicken quarters
  (thighs and drumsticks)

1 In a shallow glass or
ceramic bowl combine
tomato, tomato sauce,
wine, oil, tomato paste,
Worcestershire sauce,
Italian seasoning, and
Tabasco sauce.
2 Rinse chicken and
pat dry. Add chicken to
tomato mixture, turning
to coat. Cover;
marinate in refrigerator
for at least 1 hour,
turning occasionally.
3 Drain chicken,
reserving marinade.
Grill directly over
medium coals 25 to 30
minutes or until chicken
is tender, turning and
brushing with marinade
frequently. Garnish with
fresh chives.

Oriental Chicken

Preparation time:
  25 minutes
Marinating time:
  1 hour
Cooking time:
  25 minutes
Serves 4

1/2 cup soy sauce
1/4 cup honey
2 tablespoons sesame
  seed
2 teaspoons sesame oil
1/2 teaspoon ground
  ginger
2 cloves garlic, crushed
4 chicken quarters
  (thighs and drumsticks)

1 Combine soy sauce,
honey, sesame seed, oil,
ginger, and garlic.
2 Rinse chicken and
pat soy dry. Add chicken to
soy mixture. Cover;
marinate in refrigerator
for at least 1 hour,
turning occasionally.
3 Drain chicken,
reserving marinade.
Grill directly over
medium coals for 25 to
30 minutes or till
chicken is tender and no
longer pink, turning
and brushing with
marinade frequently.

Barbecued Satay Chicken

Preparation time:
  20 minutes
Marinating time:
  30 minutes
Cooking time:
  8 to 10 minutes
Serves 4

1 pound boneless
  skinless chicken
  thighs, in 1-inch cubes
1/3 cup chunky peanut
  butter
1 clove garlic, crushed
1 tablespoon cooking
  oil
1 tablespoon soy sauce
Pinch chili powder

1 Thread chicken onto
skewers. Place in a
shallow dish.
2 Combine peanut

HINT
Appearances are important when it comes to
buying chicken. The flesh of a fresh chicken
should be moist with no dry spots or
discoloration. The breast should be plump and
meaty. Look for a USDA Grade A mark on the
package which assures these characteristics.

Barbecued Satay Chicken

butter, garlic, oil, soy
sauce, and chili powder.
Pour over chicken.
Marinate in refrigerator
for 30 minutes.
3 Drain chicken,
reserving marinade.
Grill kabobs on an

HINT
Once chicken has been cooked, it should be
stored in the coldest part of your refrigerator
and eaten within 2 or 3 days. If the chicken
has been stuffed, remove the stuffing from the
bird and store it separately in the refrigerator
in an airtight container.

49

uncovered grill directly over medium-hot coals for 8 to 10 minutes or till chicken is tender, turning once and brushing often with reserved marinade. Serve with green salad.

Barbecued Chicken Breasts with Lime-Ginger Butter

Preparation time:
  20 minutes
Chilling time:
  30 minutes
Cooking time:
  15 to 20 minutes
Serves 6

3/4 cup butter or
  margarine
1 teaspoon finely
  shredded lime peel
2 tablespoons lime juice
2 teaspoons grated
  gingerroot
1 green onion, finely
  chopped
1/2 cup parsley, finely
  chopped
1/3 cup butter or
  margarine
6 boneless skinless
  chicken breasts
All-purpose flour

1 In a bowl beat 3/4 cup butter or margarine with an electric mixer till fluffy. Add lime peel, lime

juice, gingerroot, and green onion. Beat till well combined.
2 Shape butter mixture into a 4-inch log. Wrap in waxed paper and chill for 30 minutes. Roll butter log in chopped parsley. Rewrap and chill till serving time.
3 Dust chicken lightly with flour. Grill on an oiled grill rack directly over medium coals for 15 to 20 minutes or till chicken is tender and no longer pink, turning once.
4 Cut chilled butter log into 1/4-inch slices. Place 2 butter slices on each chicken breast and serve. The butter will melt to form a sauce.

Chicken Parcels with Honey Mustard Glaze

Preparation time:
  35 minutes
Cooking time:
  20 minutes
Serves 6 to 8

8 boneless skinless
  chicken thighs
16 pitted prunes
8 green onions, halved
  crosswise
2 tablespoons sliced
  almonds
8 slices bacon

Honey Mustard Glaze
1 tablespoon brown
  sugar
1 tablespoon Dijon
  mustard
1 tablespoon honey
1 tablespoon butter
Freshly ground pepper

1 Make a pocket in each chicken thigh by cutting to, but not through, the other side. Place 2 prunes, 2 onion halves, and a few almonds in each thigh pocket. Wrap a piece of bacon around each piece of chicken. Secure with toothpicks.
2 For glaze, combine brown sugar, mustard, honey, melted butter, and pepper.
3 Grill chicken directly over medium-slow coals for 20 minutes or till chicken is tender, turning and brushing with glaze frequently.

HINT
To make a ginger honey glaze, combine 1/2 cup soy sauce, 1/3 cup honey, and 2 teaspoons ground ginger in a small saucepan. Bring to boil, stirring constantly. Brush on chicken during the last 10 minutes of cooking. Makes about 3/4 cup.

Chicken Parcels with Honey Mustard Glaze

Special Events

The most enjoyable occasions in our lives frequently revolve around eating. Birthdays, anniversaries, and reunions demand food that complements the occasion and conjures happy memories for years to come. None of the recipes in this section are difficult (although you may need a little more time to prepare them); their "special" quality is achieved by the ingredients used — things slightly out of the ordinary that make them a cut above the rest. Dried fruits, blue cheese, choux pastry, and an array of shellfish combine wonderfully well with trusty poultry.

Chicken with Olives, Apricots, and Figs

Preparation time:
  30 minutes
Marinating time
  Overnight
Cooking time:
  1 to 1¼ hours
Serves 6

¹/₂ cup dried figs
¹/₂ cup dried apricots
¹/₂ cup pitted ripe olives
¹/₄ cup red wine
  vinegar
2 tablespoons olive oil
3 cloves garlic, crushed

1¹/₂ teaspoons dried
  thyme, crushed
1 teaspoon ground
  cumin
¹/₂ teaspoon ground
  ginger
Freshly ground pepper
3 pounds chicken pieces
¹/₄ cup dry red wine or
  orange juice
1 tablespoon brown
  sugar
Thin strips orange peel
Fresh thyme

1 In a large glass bowl combine figs, apricots, olives, vinegar, oil, garlic, thyme, cumin, and ginger. Season with pepper. Add chicken, turning to coat. Cover

Indonesian Chicken (page 54),
Chicken with Olives,
Apricots and Figs

and marinate in the refrigerator overnight, turning occasionally.

2 Transfer chicken mixture to a large shallow baking dish. Combine wine or orange juice and sugar; pour over chicken. Cover and bake in a 325° oven 30 minutes. Uncover and bake for 30 to 45 minutes more or till chicken is tender and no longer pink.

3 With a slotted spoon, transfer chicken to a serving platter. Spoon figs, apricots, and olives around chicken. Garnish with orange peel and thyme.

HINT

A "dry" marinade consists of herbs and spices rubbed into the meat. A "wet" marinade may include oils, vinegars, and citrus juices that are poured over the meat.

HINT

Make your own garam marsala by placing 2 tablespoons peppercorns, 4 teaspoons cumin seed, 1 tablespoon coriander seed, 1 teaspoon whole cardamom, and 3 inches of stick cinnamon, broken in half, in an 8 x 8 x 2-inch baking pan. Heat in a 300° oven for 15 to 20 minutes or till fragrant. Place in a spice blender or blender. Cover and blend to a fine powder. Store in an airtight container in a cool dry place. Makes about 1/3 cup.

Indonesian Chicken

Preparation time:
  20 minutes
Marinating time:
  2 hours
Cooking time:
  20 minutes
Serves 6 to 8

3 pounds chicken thighs
3 cloves garlic, crushed
2 teaspoons ground coriander
1 teaspoon brown sugar
1 teaspoon pepper
1 teaspoon ground cumin
1 teaspoon ground turmeric
3 tablespoons tamarind pulp (available at Indonesian markets)
Cooking oil

1 Trim thighs of fat. Rinse and pat dry with paper towels.
2 In a bowl combine garlic, coriander, brown sugar, pepper, cumin, and turmeric. Add tamarind pulp and stir till well combined. Rub over chicken. Cover; marinate in refrigerator at least 2 hours.
3 In a large skillet heat enough oil to cover the bottom of the skillet. Add chicken and cook over medium heat about 20 minutes or till chicken is tender and no longer pink, turning occasionally.

Chicken with Blue Cheese

Preparation time:
  30 minutes
Chilling time:
  30 minutes
Cooking time:
  5 minutes
Serves 4

4 boneless skinless chicken breasts, pounded thin
1 tablespoon chopped parsley
1 tablespoon chopped chives
3 ounces blue cheese, crumbled (see Note)
1/4 cup all-purpose flour
Freshly ground pepper
1 egg, lightly beaten
1/2 cup fine dry bread crumbs
Oil for deep-fat frying

1 Lay chicken breasts on a flat surface;

Tandoori-Style Chicken

sprinkle with parsley and chives. Divide cheese evenly over chicken. Roll up chicken and secure with toothpicks.
2 Dust chicken with flour and season with pepper. Dip chicken into egg and coat in bread crumbs. Place in refrigerator for 30 minutes.
3 Fry chicken in hot oil (375°) for 5 minutes or till golden brown. Drain on paper towels.

Note: Brie may be substituted for the blue cheese.

Tandoori-Style Chicken

Preparation time:
  20 minutes
Marinating time:
  Overnight
Cooking time:
  15 to 20 minutes
Serves 4

1 cup plain yogurt
1 tablespoon finely
  shredded lemon peel
2 tablespoons lemon
  juice
1 onion, finely
  chopped
1 clove garlic, crushed

1 teaspoon ground
  coriander
1/2 teaspoon finely
  chopped gingerroot
1/2 teaspoon ground
  cumin
1/4 teaspoon garam
  marsala (available in
  Asian markets)
4 boneless skinless
  chicken breasts

1 In a glass or ceramic bowl combine yogurt, lemon peel, lemon juice, onion, garlic, coriander, gingerroot, cumin, and garam marsala.
2 Cut chicken into 8 pieces. Add to yogurt mixture, stirring to

55

Roast Chicken in Cider

coat. Cover with plastic wrap and marinate in the refrigerator overnight.

3 Remove chicken from marinade, allowing excess to drip off. Place chicken in a baking dish. Bake in a 425° oven for 15 to 20 minutes or till chicken is tender and no longer pink. Serve with rice and sambals (see Note).

Note: Sambals are small side dishes such as onion, cucumber and yogurt, banana and

coconut, and mango chutney. Serve several to complement the rich spicy flavors.

HINT
Packaged stuffing mixes are useful when you're in a hurry. Use them as the base for your own creations. Stir in shredded orange or lemon peel, chopped parsley, chopped nuts, or chopped celery leaves for extra flavor.

Roast Chicken in Cider

Preparation time:
  35 minutes
Cooking time:
  1 1/2 hours
Serves 4

4 slices bacon, cut into
  thin strips
2 1/2- to 3-pound whole
  chicken
1/4 cup butter or
  margarine
1 white onion, cut into
  thin wedges

1 cup apple cider
1 cup homemade chicken stock or canned broth
2 bay leaves
1/2 teaspoon dried thyme, crushed
Freshly ground pepper
6 medium carrots
4 medium potatoes
Chopped parsley

1 In a large skillet cook bacon till light brown. Transfer with a slotted spoon to a shallow baking dish, reserving bacon drippings.
2 Rinse chicken and pat dry with paper towels. Fold back wings and tie legs together. Add butter or margarine to bacon drippings in skillet and heat over medium heat. Add chicken to skillet and brown on all sides. Place on top of bacon in baking dish.
3 In same skillet cook onion in drippings till tender. Sprinkle onion over chicken. Add cider, chicken stock, bay leaves, and thyme. Season with pepper.
4 Bake, uncovered, in a 350° oven for 30 minutes. Meanwhile, peel carrots and potatoes; cut into chunks. Add carrots and potatoes to chicken. Bake for 1 hour more or till chicken is tender and

no longer pink and vegetables are done, basting frequently with pan juices and turning vegetables occasionally.
5 Cut chicken into quarters and sprinkle with parsley. Serve vegetables with chicken.

Note: If necessary, cover chicken with foil during the last part of cooking to prevent overbrowning.

Chicken Curry with Cashews and Almonds

Preparation time:
  30 minutes
Cooking time:
  45 minutes
Serves 6

1/3 cup cooking oil
2 large onions, finely chopped
4 cloves garlic, crushed
1 tablespoon finely chopped gingerroot
2 tablespoons garam marsala (available at Asian markets)
1 tablespoon ground coriander
1 teaspoon ground turmeric
14 1/2-ounce can chopped tomatoes
3 pounds chicken pieces, skinned

1 tablespoon finely chopped fresh mint
1/2 cup plain yogurt
1/2 cup unsalted cashews
1/2 cup almonds, coarsely chopped

1 In a large skillet heat oil. Cook onion in oil till tender and brown. Add garlic and gingerroot. Cook and stir for 2 minutes. Add garam marsala, ground coriander, and turmeric. Cook and stir 2 minutes.
2 Stir in undrained tomatoes. Add chicken and mint. Bring to a boil; reduce heat. Cook, uncovered, about 45 minutes or till chicken is tender and no longer pink, stirring occasionally to prevent sticking. (Add a little water if sticking occurs).
3 Stir yogurt and nuts into chicken mixture. Heat through.

> **HINT**
> Roast chicken with stuffing makes a great meal, but sometimes the stuffing spills out of the bird during cooking. Prevent this by placing a piece of day old bread rubbed with garlic in the cavity opening before roasting.

Chicken and Broccoli Gougère

Preparation time:
  40 minutes
Cooking time:
  30 minutes
Serves 6

*2 large boneless skinless
  chicken breasts
9- or 10-ounce package
  frozen broccoli
  flowerets
1 cup shredded sharp
  cheddar cheese
2 tablespoons
  cornstarch
1 cup milk
Freshly ground pepper
1 cup water
1/2 cup butter
1 cup all-purpose flour
4 eggs*

1 In a skillet cook
chicken breasts in
simmering water for
12 to 14 minutes or till
tender. Drain and cool.
Cut into strips. Set aside.
2 Cook broccoli
according to package
directions; drain. In a
bowl combine shredded
cheese and cornstarch.
In a medium saucepan
heat milk to simmering.
Gradually add cheese
mixture, stirring
constantly. Allow
cheese to melt between
each addition. Season
with pepper. Stir in
chicken and broccoli.

*Chicken Curry with Cashews and
Almonds (page 57), Chicken and Broccoli Gougè*

58

3 In a small saucepan combine water and butter. Bring to a boil; remove from heat. Add flour all at once, beating with a wooden spoon. Return to heat; stir till mixture is smooth and comes away from the side of the pan. Cool slightly.

4 Add eggs, one at a time, to flour mixture, beating well after each addition till smooth. Drop batter by tablespoonsful around the sides of a greased 10-inch dish, leaving the middle empty. Pour chicken mixture into empty space in middle.

5 Bake in a 400° oven 30 minutes or till pastry puffs and turns golden brown. Serve at once.

Roast Spiced Cornish Hens

Preparation time:
 30 minutes
Cooking time:
 1¹/₂ hours
Serves 6

3 frozen Cornish game hens, thawed
3 tablespoons honey
2 tablespoons cooking oil
1 tablespoon rosewater
1 tablespoon lemon juice
2 teaspoons ground cardamom
¹/₂ teaspoon salt
Pinch ground red pepper
¹/₂ cup blanched almonds
Fresh coriander or cilantro

1 Rinse hens and pat dry with paper towels. In a bowl combine honey, oil, rosewater, lemon juice, cardamom, salt, and ground red pepper.

2 Line a baking sheet with a piece of foil large enough to wrap around the hens. Place hens on foil. Pour a little honey mixture into cavity of each hen. Pour remaining honey mixture over hens and sprinkle with almonds.

3 Bring foil up around hens and seal by folding over the edges. Bake in a 350° oven for 1 hour. Unwrap and spoon cooking juices over hens. Roast, uncovered, for 30 minutes more or till golden brown, tender, basting with cooking juices occasionally.

4 Let stand 5 minutes. Serve with almonds and garnish with fresh coriander or cilantro.

Roast Spiced Cornish Hens

HINT
In hot weather, nuts can quickly turn rancid. Buy them in small amounts and store in an airtight container in a cool dry place. Or place them in the freezer and store for several months.

Pecan Chicken

Pecan Chicken

Preparation time:
30 minutes
Cooking time:
6 to 8 minutes
Serves 4

4 boneless skinless
   chicken breasts
1 cup pecan halves
1/2 cup shredded Gouda
   cheese
1/2 cup fine dry bread
   crumbs
1/2 cup soft bread crumbs
1 teaspoon ground sage
Freshly ground pepper
1 egg, lightly beaten
1 tablespoon water
1/4 cup butter margarine
2 tablespoons cooking oil
Fresh watercress

1 Place chicken
between 2 pieces plastic
wrap. Pound with the
flat side of a meat
mallet till about
1/2-inch thick.
2 Reserve 8 pecan
halves. Finely chop
remaining pecans.
In a shallow bowl
combine chopped
pecans, cheese, bread
crumbs, and sage.
Season with pepper. In
another shallow bowl
combine egg and water.
3 Coat chicken with

pecan mixture. Dip in
egg mixture and coat
with more pecan
mixture.
4 In a large skillet
heat butter and oil over
medium heat. Place
2 chicken breasts in
skillet and cook for 2 to
3 minutes on each side
or till brown, tender,
and no longer pink.
Keep chicken warm
while cooking the
remaining pieces.
Garnish with fresh
watercress.

HINT
Turkey breast tenderloin slices can substitute for
boneless skinless chicken breasts. For Pecan
Chicken, you won't need to pound the turkey if
you buy the thin slices of turkey tenderloin
available in the meat cases at most supermarkets.

Spanish Paella

Preparation time:
40 minutes
Cooking time:
1 hour
Serves 4

2¹/₂- to 3-pound
  chicken, cut up
2 cloves garlic, finely
  chopped
1 tablespoon olive oil
1 medium onion,
  chopped
1¹/₄ cups long grain
  rice
3¹/₄ cups homemade
  chicken stock or
  canned broth
6 saffron threads
12 ounces prawns or
  large shrimp, peeled
  and deveined
2 red bell peppers, cut
  into 1-inch squares
1¹/₂ cups frozen peas
12 to 16 small mussels
Water or dry white
  wine

1 In a large oven-going skillet heat oil. Brown chicken in hot oil. Add garlic, cook for 2 minutes. Remove chicken.
2 In skillet cook onion till tender. Add rice; cook and stir till golden brown. Add chicken stock and saffron. Bring to a boil. Return chicken to skillet. Cover and remove from heat.
3 Place covered skillet in oven and bake at 375° for 45 minutes. Add prawns or shrimp, bell pepper, and frozen peas. Cover, to bake for 15 to 20 minutes more or till rice is tender and liquid is absorbed.
4 Scrub and debeard mussels. Place in saucepan with little water or wine. Bring to boil; reduce heat. Cover, simmer 3 minutes or till shells open. Discard any unopened shells.
5 Fluff rice with a fork and top with mussels.

1. For Spanish Paella, brown chicken pieces in hot oil.

2. Cook onion and rice in pan juices until onion is tender and rice is golden brown.